Cape Verde

Everything You Need to Know

Introduction to Cape Verde

Nestled in the Atlantic Ocean, off the coast of West Africa, lies the captivating archipelago of Cape Verde. Comprising ten volcanic islands and several islets, Cape Verde is a testament to nature's artistic prowess. Each island boasts its unique charm, offering visitors a diverse tapestry of landscapes, cultures, and experiences. From the sun-kissed beaches of Sal and Boa Vista to the rugged peaks of Santo Antão and Fogo, Cape Verde is a paradise for adventurers and relaxation-seekers alike.

With a history steeped in colonialism and resilience, Cape Verde has evolved into a vibrant melting pot of cultures. Its strategic location made it a crucial stop along the transatlantic slave trade route, leaving an indelible mark on its cultural heritage. The islands' rich blend of African, European, and Creole influences is evident in its music, cuisine, and language.

Cape Verde gained independence from Portuguese colonial rule in 1975, marking a new chapter in its history. Since then, the archipelago has made significant strides in economic development, governance, and social progress. Despite facing challenges such as droughts and economic disparities, Cape Verdeans have demonstrated remarkable resilience and determination in building a brighter future for their nation.

Today, Cape Verde stands as a beacon of stability and democracy in Africa, garnering praise for its commitment to human rights and good governance. Its thriving tourism industry, bolstered by pristine beaches, vibrant culture, and warm hospitality, has positioned it as a sought-after destination for travelers from around the globe.

As we embark on this journey through the enchanting islands of Cape Verde, we invite you to delve into its rich history, explore its breathtaking landscapes, savor its unique flavors, and immerse yourself in the warmth of its people. Join us as we uncover the hidden treasures and timeless beauty of this Atlantic gem. Welcome to Cape Verde.

The Geographical Marvel: Exploring Cape Verde's Islands

Nestled in the Atlantic Ocean, off the coast of West Africa, the archipelago of Cape Verde is a geographical marvel waiting to be explored. Consisting of ten main islands and several smaller islets, each boasting its own unique character and allure, Cape Verde offers a diverse range of landscapes and experiences to visitors.

The islands of Cape Verde are of volcanic origin, formed millions of years ago through volcanic activity. This volcanic heritage is evident in the rugged terrain and dramatic landscapes that characterize many of the islands. From towering peaks to lush valleys, Cape Verde's geography is as diverse as it is breathtaking.

Among the most notable islands is Fogo, home to the imposing Pico do Fogo, a volcano that rises over 2,800 meters above sea level. The volcano last erupted in 2014, leaving behind a lunar-like landscape of lava fields and ash-covered slopes. Despite its destructive potential, the volcano is also a source of fertility, with the rich volcanic soil supporting agriculture on the island.

Santo Antão, known as the "green island" due to its lush vegetation, offers a stark contrast to the arid landscapes of some of its neighbors. Here, visitors can explore verdant valleys, cascading waterfalls, and terraced hillsides dotted with banana plantations and sugarcane fields.

Sal and Boa Vista, on the other hand, are renowned for their pristine beaches and turquoise waters. These islands attract sunseekers and water sports enthusiasts from around the world, offering a wealth of opportunities for swimming, snorkeling, windsurfing, and kiteboarding.

São Vicente, home to the vibrant port city of Mindelo, is known for its lively cultural scene and cosmopolitan atmosphere. With its colonial architecture, bustling markets, and lively music festivals, Mindelo offers visitors a taste of Cape Verdean urban life.

Other islands, such as Santiago, the largest and most populous island, offer a blend of historical sites, vibrant cities, and stunning natural beauty. Here, visitors can explore the colonial-era capital city of Praia, visit historic landmarks such as the Cidade Velha, a UNESCO World Heritage Site, and trek through lush mountain ranges and fertile valleys.

Whether you're seeking adventure, relaxation, or cultural immersion, Cape Verde's islands have something to offer everyone. From the rugged peaks of Fogo to the sandy shores of Sal, each island beckons with its own unique charm and allure. So pack your bags, and get ready to embark on an unforgettable journey through this captivating archipelago.

Colonial Roots: Tracing Cape Verde's History

To truly understand Cape Verde's history, we must delve into its colonial roots, a story that intertwines with the broader narrative of European expansion and exploitation in Africa. The archipelago's history is deeply intertwined with Portuguese colonialism, with the first European explorers arriving in the 15th century. These early explorers, including Diogo Gomes and António de Noli, were drawn to Cape Verde's strategic location as a stopping point on the transatlantic slave trade route.

By the 16th century, Portuguese settlers had established permanent colonies on the islands, using them as a base for trade, agriculture, and, unfortunately, the transatlantic slave trade. Cape Verde became a crucial hub in the triangular trade network, with enslaved Africans being transported from the continent to the Americas via the islands.

Throughout the colonial period, Cape Verde served as a center for the transshipment of goods and people between Europe, Africa, and the Americas. The islands' strategic location made them a coveted possession for European powers, leading to conflicts and power struggles over control of the archipelago.

Despite the harsh conditions of colonial rule, Cape Verdeans developed a distinct culture and identity shaped by their African, European, and Creole heritage. The islands became a melting pot of cultures, languages, and traditions, with Cape Verdean Creole emerging as a unique blend of Portuguese and African languages.

In 1975, after centuries of colonial rule, Cape Verde finally gained independence from Portugal, marking a new chapter in its history. Since then, the archipelago has undergone significant social, political, and economic transformations as it seeks to forge its own path as a sovereign nation.

Today, Cape Verdeans look back on their colonial past with a mixture of pride and sorrow, acknowledging the resilience of their ancestors in the face of oppression and exploitation. As the nation continues to navigate the complexities of post-colonialism, it remains rooted in its history while embracing the opportunities and challenges of the future.

Independence and Beyond: Modern Cape Verde

With the dawn of independence in 1975, Cape Verde stepped into a new era, marked by hope, determination, and the promise of self-determination. Breaking free from centuries of Portuguese colonial rule, the archipelago embarked on a journey of nation-building, navigating the complexities of post-colonialism while charting its own course as a sovereign nation.

In the early years of independence, Cape Verde faced a myriad of challenges, including economic instability, political uncertainty, and social unrest. However, despite these obstacles, the fledgling nation remained steadfast in its commitment to democracy, human rights, and economic development.

Throughout the latter half of the 20th century and into the 21st century, Cape Verde experienced significant progress and growth across various sectors. The government implemented policies aimed at diversifying the economy, reducing poverty, and improving infrastructure, leading to steady economic growth and development.

One of the key drivers of Cape Verde's economic success has been the growth of its tourism industry. Blessed with pristine beaches, vibrant culture, and warm hospitality, the archipelago has become a popular destination for travelers seeking sun, sea, and relaxation. Tourism has emerged as a vital source of revenue, driving job creation, infrastructure development, and economic growth across the islands.

In addition to tourism, Cape Verde has also made strides in other sectors, including agriculture, fisheries, and renewable energy. The government has invested in initiatives to promote sustainable development, harnessing the islands' natural resources while preserving their fragile ecosystems.

Politically, Cape Verde has earned a reputation as a beacon of stability and democracy in Africa. The country holds regular elections, enjoys freedom of speech and press, and upholds the rule of law. Cape Verde has also played an active role in regional and international affairs, advocating for peace, security, and development in Africa and beyond.

Socially, Cape Verde has made progress in areas such as education, healthcare, and gender equality. The government has invested in expanding access to education and healthcare services, improving literacy rates, and reducing infant mortality. Efforts to promote gender equality have also been underway, with initiatives aimed at empowering women and girls and combating gender-based violence.

As Cape Verde looks to the future, it faces new challenges and opportunities on the horizon. From climate change and environmental sustainability to economic diversification and social inclusion, the archipelago continues to evolve and adapt in a rapidly changing world. Yet, through it all, Cape Verde remains anchored in its rich history, vibrant culture, and enduring spirit of resilience.

A Tapestry of Cultures: Diversity in Cape Verde

Cape Verde is a melting pot of cultures, a vibrant tapestry woven together by centuries of history, migration, and intermingling. Situated at the crossroads of Africa, Europe, and the Americas, the archipelago has been shaped by a diverse array of influences, each leaving its mark on the islands' rich cultural heritage.

The roots of Cape Verde's cultural mosaic can be traced back to its early history, when Portuguese explorers first set foot on the islands in the 15th century. These early settlers brought with them their language, religion, and customs, laying the foundation for Cape Verdean society. Over time, as the islands became a hub for the transatlantic slave trade, African, European, and indigenous cultures converged, giving rise to a unique blend of traditions and identities.

One of the most significant cultural influences in Cape Verde is that of Africa, particularly the regions of West Africa from which many of the islands' inhabitants are descended. African cultural elements are evident in Cape Verdean music, dance, cuisine, and religious practices, reflecting the resilience and creativity of the islands' African ancestors.

European influence, particularly Portuguese, also plays a prominent role in Cape Verdean culture. Portuguese colonization brought with it the Portuguese language, Catholicism, and European customs and traditions, which have become deeply ingrained in Cape Verdean society. However, Cape Verdeans have adapted and transformed these influences, infusing them with their own unique flavor and character.

In addition to African and European influences, Cape Verdean culture also bears the imprint of other cultures, including indigenous peoples and immigrants from other parts of the world. The islands' strategic location made them a melting pot of cultures, attracting settlers, traders, and explorers from Africa, Europe, and beyond.

Today, Cape Verdean culture is a dynamic and ever-evolving tapestry, reflecting the diverse backgrounds and experiences of its people. From the rhythms of morna and coladeira to the flavors of cachupa and pastel de milho, Cape Verdean culture is a celebration of diversity, resilience, and creativity. It is this unique blend of influences that makes Cape Verde a truly special and captivating destination, where visitors can immerse themselves in a world of music, dance, and flavors unlike any other.

Creole Culture: Language and Identity

Creole culture lies at the heart of Cape Verdean identity, shaping the way its people communicate, express themselves, and connect with one another. At the core of this culture is Cape Verdean Creole, a unique language born out of the islands' complex history of colonization, slavery, and cultural exchange.

Cape Verdean Creole, also known as Kriolu or Kriol, is a creole language that evolved from a blend of Portuguese, African languages, and other European and indigenous influences. It emerged as a means of communication among the diverse populations of the islands, bridging linguistic and cultural divides and creating a sense of unity and belonging among Cape Verdeans.

The origins of Cape Verdean Creole can be traced back to the early days of Portuguese colonization, when European settlers and African slaves were brought together on the islands. Over time, as these disparate groups interacted and intermarried, a new language began to emerge, incorporating elements of Portuguese grammar and vocabulary with African linguistic structures and influences.

18

Today, Cape Verdean Creole is spoken by the majority of Cape Verdeans as their first language, alongside Portuguese, which serves as the official language of the country. While Portuguese is used in government, education, and formal settings, Cape Verdean Creole remains the language of everyday communication, culture, and identity for most Cape Verdeans.

Cape Verdean Creole is a testament to the resilience and creativity of the islands' people, reflecting their ability to adapt and innovate in the face of adversity. It is a living language, constantly evolving and changing, with different dialects and variations spoken on each of the islands.

In addition to its linguistic significance, Cape Verdean Creole also plays a central role in shaping Cape Verdean culture and identity. It is the language of Cape Verdean music, poetry, and literature, serving as a medium for artistic expression and cultural preservation. Through its rich vocabulary, expressive intonation, and rhythmic cadence, Cape Verdean Creole captures the spirit and soul of the islands, conveying a sense of belonging and solidarity among its speakers.

In recent years, efforts have been made to promote and preserve Cape Verdean Creole as a vital component of Cape Verdean heritage. Schools have introduced Cape Verdean Creole into their curriculum, and initiatives have been launched to document and archive the language for future generations. As Cape Verde continues to evolve and grow, Cape Verdean Creole remains a cornerstone of its cultural identity, connecting its people to their past, present, and future.

The Melting Pot of Music: Cape Verdean Rhythms

When it comes to music, Cape Verde is a vibrant melting pot of rhythms, melodies, and beats that reflect the rich cultural heritage of the islands. From the soulful strains of morna to the infectious rhythms of funaná and coladeira, Cape Verdean music is as diverse and dynamic as the people who create it.

At the heart of Cape Verdean music is morna, a genre often described as the soul of Cape Verde. Characterized by its melancholic melodies and heartfelt lyrics, morna is a genre that speaks to the joys and sorrows of life on the islands. Originating in the 19th century, morna has its roots in Portuguese fado and African rhythms, blending elements of both to create a uniquely Cape Verdean sound. Legendary singer Cesária Évora, known as the "Barefoot Diva," brought morna to international prominence with her emotive performances and velvety voice.

In addition to morna, Cape Verde is also known for its lively dance music, including funaná and coladeira. Funaná, characterized by its upbeat tempo and accordion-driven melodies, originated among the rural communities of Santiago and São Vicente. It was traditionally played at festive occasions such as weddings and harvest celebrations, where it served as a form of communal expression and celebration. Coladeira, on the other hand, is a more urban genre, with influences ranging from Brazilian samba to Caribbean zouk. Known for its catchy rhythms and playful lyrics, coladeira is a popular dance music that gets people moving and grooving on the dance floor.

Cape Verdean music is also deeply rooted in the islands' African heritage, with rhythms and instruments that trace their origins back to the African continent. Percussion instruments such as the tambor, ferrinho, and cavaquinho are commonly used in traditional Cape Verdean music, adding layers of texture and depth to the sound.

In recent years, Cape Verdean music has gained international recognition, with artists such as Mayra Andrade, Lura, and Tito Paris bringing the sounds of the islands to audiences around the world. Cape Verdean music festivals, such as the Kriol Jazz Festival and Festival de Gamboa, attract music lovers from far and wide, showcasing the talents of local and international artists alike.

Whether it's the soulful melodies of morna, the infectious rhythms of funaná, or the playful beats of coladeira, Cape Verdean music captivates the senses and stirs the soul, reflecting the beauty, complexity, and resilience of Cape Verdean culture.

Culinary Traditions: Tasting Cape Verde's Flavors

Exploring Cape Verde's culinary traditions is a journey into a world of vibrant flavors, rich spices, and hearty dishes that reflect the islands' diverse cultural heritage. From succulent seafood to hearty stews and tropical fruits, Cape Verdean cuisine is a delicious fusion of African, European, and indigenous influences.

One of the staples of Cape Verdean cuisine is cachupa, a hearty stew made with corn, beans, vegetables, and meat or fish. It's often simmered for hours, allowing the flavors to meld together and create a comforting and satisfying dish that's enjoyed by locals and visitors alike. Cachupa is considered the national dish of Cape Verde, and each island has its own variation, with ingredients and seasonings varying depending on local tastes and traditions.

Seafood is abundant in Cape Verde, thanks to the islands' rich marine biodiversity. Freshly caught fish such as tuna, grouper, and snapper are grilled, fried, or stewed and served with flavorful sauces and accompaniments. Lobster, shrimp, and shellfish are also popular choices, often prepared simply to let the natural flavors shine through.

Another highlight of Cape Verdean cuisine is pastel de milho, a savory cornmeal cake that's similar to Italian polenta. It's often served as a side dish or snack, accompanied by fish, meat, or vegetables. Pastel de milho is versatile and can be cooked in various ways, including frying, baking, or steaming, depending on personal preference.

No exploration of Cape Verdean cuisine would be complete without sampling its tropical fruits. Mangoes, papayas, guavas, and bananas are just a few of the fruits that thrive in the islands' warm climate, providing a burst of freshness and sweetness to any meal. These fruits are often enjoyed fresh or incorporated into desserts, juices, and smoothies.

In addition to its traditional dishes, Cape Verdean cuisine also features a variety of breads, pastries, and sweets. Pão, or bread, is a staple of Cape Verdean meals, often served alongside stews or used to make sandwiches. Bolo de coco, or coconut cake, is a popular dessert made with grated coconut, sugar, and eggs, baked to perfection and enjoyed with a cup of coffee or tea.

Overall, Cape Verdean cuisine is a celebration of flavors, textures, and aromas that reflect the islands' rich cultural heritage and natural abundance. Whether you're savoring a bowl of cachupa, indulging in fresh seafood, or enjoying a slice of coconut cake, each bite tells a story of tradition, innovation, and the spirit of Cape Verde.

From Sea to Plate: Fishing in Cape Verde

Fishing is not just a livelihood in Cape Verde; it's a way of life deeply rooted in the islands' culture and history. With its vast marine resources and strategic location in the Atlantic Ocean, Cape Verde has long been a paradise for fishermen and seafood enthusiasts alike.

From the bustling fishing ports of Mindelo and Praia to the remote coastal villages scattered across the islands, fishing is an integral part of Cape Verdean society. It provides sustenance, employment, and a sense of community for thousands of Cape Verdeans who rely on the sea for their livelihoods.

Traditional fishing methods, such as handline fishing and net casting, are still practiced by many Cape Verdean fishermen today, alongside modern techniques such as longlining and trawling. These methods vary depending on the type of fish being targeted, the location of the fishing grounds, and the preferences of individual fishermen.

One of the most prized catches in Cape Verdean waters is tuna, particularly yellowfin tuna, which is abundant in the islands' warm and nutrient-rich waters. Tuna fishing is a major industry in

Cape Verde, with large fleets of commercial fishing vessels plying the seas in search of these prized fish. Tuna is not only a valuable export commodity but also a staple food source for Cape Verdeans, who enjoy it fresh, grilled, or canned.

In addition to tuna, Cape Verdean waters are home to a wide variety of fish species, including grouper, snapper, mackerel, and barracuda. Shellfish such as lobster, shrimp, and crab are also plentiful, providing a rich and diverse seafood bounty for fishermen and consumers alike.

Despite the abundance of marine resources, Cape Verdean fishermen face challenges such as overfishing, illegal fishing, and environmental degradation. Climate change, pollution, and habitat destruction pose additional threats to the sustainability of Cape Verde's fisheries, putting the livelihoods of fishermen and the food security of the islands at risk.

In response to these challenges, the Cape Verdean government has implemented measures to promote sustainable fishing practices, protect marine ecosystems, and ensure the long-term viability of the fishing industry. These efforts include the establishment of marine protected areas, the implementation of fishing quotas and regulations, and the promotion of alternative livelihoods for fishing communities.

Despite the challenges they face, Cape Verdean fishermen continue to cast their nets and lines into the sea, drawing sustenance and inspiration from the bountiful waters that surround their islands. Fishing in Cape Verde is more than just a means of putting food on the table; it's a timeless tradition, a source of pride, and a vital link between the people and the sea.

Agricultural Heritage: Farming on the Islands

Farming in Cape Verde is a testament to human ingenuity and perseverance in the face of adversity. The islands' rugged terrain, arid climate, and limited freshwater resources pose significant challenges to agriculture, yet Cape Verdeans have developed innovative techniques and practices to cultivate the land and sustain their communities.

Historically, agriculture has played a central role in Cape Verdean society, providing food, employment, and economic stability for generations of islanders. Traditional farming methods, such as terracing, irrigation, and crop rotation, have been used for centuries to maximize the productivity of the islands' limited arable land.

One of the most iconic features of Cape Verdean agriculture is its system of terraced fields, known as poios. These stone-walled terraces are built into the hillsides, creating flat, level surfaces for planting crops and preventing soil erosion. Poios are used to cultivate a variety of crops, including maize, beans, sweet potatoes, and cassava, as well as fruits such as bananas, papayas, and mangoes.

Water scarcity is a significant challenge for farmers in Cape Verde, with the islands receiving limited rainfall and relying heavily on irrigation for crop production. To overcome this challenge, Cape Verdeans have developed innovative water management techniques, such as building cisterns, reservoirs, and catchment systems to capture and store rainwater for agricultural use.

In addition to traditional farming methods, Cape Verdeans have also embraced modern agricultural practices, such as greenhouse farming, hydroponics, and agroforestry. These techniques allow farmers to grow a wider variety of crops, increase yields, and conserve water and soil resources.

Despite these efforts, agriculture in Cape Verde faces numerous challenges, including soil degradation, desertification, and climate change. Rising temperatures, unpredictable rainfall patterns, and extreme weather events threaten the viability of farming on the islands, making it increasingly difficult for farmers to sustain their livelihoods.

In response to these challenges, the Cape Verdean government has implemented programs and initiatives to support sustainable agriculture, promote soil conservation, and increase food security. These efforts include the development of drought-resistant crop varieties, the expansion of irrigation infrastructure, and the promotion of organic farming practices.

Despite the challenges they face, Cape Verdean farmers remain resilient and resourceful, adapting to changing conditions and finding innovative solutions to sustain their communities. Farming in Cape Verde is not just a means of producing food; it's a way of life, a connection to the land, and a testament to the human spirit's ability to thrive in even the harshest of environments.

Biodiversity Hotspot: Wildlife of Cape Verde

Cape Verde's wildlife is as diverse and unique as the islands themselves, with a wealth of endemic species found nowhere else on Earth. Despite its relatively small size and isolated location, Cape Verde is considered a biodiversity hotspot, boasting a rich array of flora and fauna that have adapted to the islands' distinct ecosystems.

One of the most iconic species of Cape Verde is the loggerhead sea turtle, which nests on the islands' sandy beaches during the nesting season. These majestic creatures, known for their distinctive ridged shells and powerful flippers, are a symbol of conservation and environmental stewardship in Cape Verde.

In addition to sea turtles, Cape Verde is home to a variety of marine life, including dolphins, whales, and sharks. The islands' warm waters provide vital habitat for these marine species, which are often spotted by tourists and locals alike on boat tours and diving expeditions.

On land, Cape Verde is inhabited by a variety of bird species, many of which are endemic to the islands. The Cape Verde warbler, Cape Verde swift, and Cape Verde buzzard are just a few examples of the avian diversity found on the islands. These birds play important roles in the islands' ecosystems, serving as pollinators, seed dispersers, and indicators of environmental health.

Cape Verde's terrestrial fauna also includes a number of reptiles and amphibians, such as geckos, skinks, and frogs. These creatures have adapted to the islands' dry, rocky terrain, using camouflage, burrowing, and other survival strategies to thrive in their harsh environment.

In terms of flora, Cape Verde is home to a variety of plant species, many of which are found only on specific islands or habitats. The islands' native vegetation includes succulent plants, shrubs, and grasses, which have evolved to survive in the islands' arid climate and nutrient-poor soils.

Unfortunately, Cape Verde's unique biodiversity is facing threats from habitat loss, invasive species, and climate change. Human activities such as deforestation, overfishing, and development are putting pressure on the islands' fragile ecosystems, endangering the survival of many native species.

In response to these threats, the Cape Verdean government and local conservation organizations have implemented measures to protect and preserve the islands' wildlife and natural habitats. These efforts include the establishment of protected areas, conservation programs, and public awareness campaigns aimed at promoting sustainable development and environmental stewardship.

Despite the challenges they face, Cape Verde's wildlife and natural beauty continue to inspire awe and admiration among visitors and locals alike. From the sandy shores to the rugged mountains, the islands' ecosystems are a testament to the resilience and diversity of life on Earth.

Unique Ecosystems: Exploring Cape Verde's Natural Reserves

Exploring Cape Verde's natural reserves is a journey into some of the most unique and diverse ecosystems on Earth. Despite its small size, the archipelago is home to a remarkable variety of habitats, from lush valleys and verdant mountains to arid deserts and rocky coastlines.

One of the most iconic natural reserves in Cape Verde is the Parque Natural do Fogo, located on the island of Fogo. This protected area encompasses the dramatic landscapes of the island's volcanic peak, Pico do Fogo, as well as its surrounding forests, craters, and lava fields. Visitors to the park can hike through ancient lava flows, explore volcanic caves, and witness the breathtaking vistas from the summit of Pico do Fogo.

On the island of Santo Antão, the Parque Natural de Cova offers a glimpse into the island's lush and rugged interior. This protected area encompasses the Cova crater, a verdant valley surrounded by towering peaks and cascading waterfalls. Hikers and nature enthusiasts can traverse the park's scenic trails, passing through forests of endemic plants, crossing mountain streams, and soaking in the panoramic views of the island's dramatic landscapes.

In addition to its terrestrial reserves, Cape Verde is also home to several marine protected areas, which safeguard the islands' rich marine biodiversity. The Reserva Natural de Santa Luzia, located off the coast of São Vicente, is one such reserve, protecting the pristine coral reefs, seagrass beds, and marine habitats surrounding the uninhabited island of Santa Luzia. These protected areas provide vital habitat for a variety of marine species, including endangered sea turtles, dolphins, and sharks.

Cape Verde's natural reserves are not only important for conservation but also for eco-tourism, offering visitors the opportunity to experience the islands' unique ecosystems firsthand. Whether hiking through volcanic landscapes, snorkeling among coral reefs, or birdwatching in lush forests, exploring Cape Verde's natural reserves is a journey of discovery and wonder, showcasing the beauty and diversity of this Atlantic gem.

White Sands and Azure Waters: Cape Verde's Beaches

Cape Verde is blessed with some of the most stunning beaches in the world, each offering its own unique blend of white sands and azure waters. From secluded coves to bustling resort towns, the islands' coastline boasts a wealth of beaches that cater to every taste and preference.

Sal and Boa Vista, two of the most popular tourist destinations in Cape Verde, are renowned for their pristine beaches and crystal-clear waters. The beaches of Sal, such as Santa Maria Beach and Kite Beach, are perfect for sunbathing, swimming, and water sports, with soft white sands and gentle waves lapping against the shore. Boa Vista's beaches, including Praia de Chaves and Praia de Santa Monica, are equally breathtaking, with miles of untouched coastline and dramatic sand dunes stretching as far as the eye can see.

In addition to Sal and Boa Vista, other islands in Cape Verde also boast beautiful beaches worth exploring. São Vicente's São Pedro Beach is a favorite among locals and visitors alike, with its vibrant atmosphere, colorful fishing boats, and sweeping views of the ocean. Santiago's Tarrafal Beach offers a more laid-back experience, with its calm waters and shady palm trees providing the perfect setting for a relaxing day by the sea.

For those seeking adventure, Cape Verde's beaches offer a wide range of water sports and activities to enjoy. From kiteboarding and windsurfing to snorkeling and diving, there's something for everyone to enjoy in the islands' warm and inviting waters. And for nature lovers, the beaches of Cape Verde are also home to a variety of marine life, including colorful fish, sea turtles, and dolphins, making them ideal for wildlife viewing and exploration.

Whether you're looking for relaxation, adventure, or simply a stunning backdrop for your vacation photos, Cape Verde's beaches have it all. With their pristine sands, turquoise waters, and endless sunshine, these beaches are the perfect escape for anyone seeking a slice of paradise in the heart of the Atlantic Ocean.

Adventures in the Atlantic: Water Sports and Activities

Embarking on adventures in the Atlantic waters surrounding Cape Verde is an exhilarating experience that offers a plethora of water sports and activities for enthusiasts of all kinds. With its warm, clear waters and steady trade winds, Cape Verde is a paradise for water lovers, offering a wide range of activities to suit every taste and skill level.

One of the most popular water sports in Cape Verde is kiteboarding, thanks to the island's consistent winds and wide-open beaches. Sal and Boa Vista are particularly well-known for their kiteboarding conditions, attracting enthusiasts from around the world to ride the waves and catch the wind. Whether you're a beginner looking to take lessons or an experienced rider seeking new challenges, Cape Verde's kiteboarding spots offer endless opportunities for fun and excitement.

Windsurfing is another beloved water sport in Cape Verde, with its roots tracing back to the islands' Portuguese and African heritage. With its steady trade winds and flat water conditions, Cape Verde provides the perfect playground for windsurfers of all levels. Beginners can take lessons in sheltered bays, while more experienced riders can tackle the waves and ramps along the coast.

For those who prefer a more relaxed pace, snorkeling and diving offer a chance to explore Cape Verde's vibrant underwater world. The islands' clear waters are home to a variety of marine life, including colorful fish, sea turtles, and coral reefs. Snorkelers and divers can explore underwater caves, swim with dolphins, and discover hidden shipwrecks, making for unforgettable underwater adventures.

Fishing is another popular activity in Cape Verde, with opportunities to catch a variety of species, including tuna, marlin, and barracuda. Whether you're casting a line from shore or heading out to sea on a fishing charter, Cape Verde's rich marine biodiversity ensures a rewarding and memorable fishing experience.

In addition to these activities, Cape Verde also offers opportunities for sailing, kayaking, paddleboarding, and more. Whether you're gliding along the coast in a sailboat, exploring hidden coves in a kayak, or riding the waves on a stand-up paddleboard, there's no shortage of ways to enjoy the beauty and excitement of Cape Verde's Atlantic waters.

With its endless array of water sports and activities, Cape Verde is a playground for adventure seekers and water enthusiasts alike. Whether you're seeking thrills, relaxation, or simply a chance to connect with nature, the islands' warm waters and sunny skies offer endless possibilities for unforgettable experiences on the water.

Sal: Gateway to Cape Verde's Tourism

Sal, often referred to as the "Gateway to Cape Verde's Tourism," is one of the most popular destinations in the archipelago, attracting visitors with its stunning beaches, vibrant culture, and array of recreational activities. Located in the northern part of the Cape Verdean archipelago, Sal is renowned for its year-round sunshine, warm temperatures, and inviting waters, making it an ideal destination for beach lovers and outdoor enthusiasts alike.

The island's main town, Santa Maria, serves as the hub of tourism on Sal, offering a lively atmosphere with its colorful buildings, bustling markets, and array of restaurants, bars, and shops. Visitors can stroll along the picturesque seafront promenade, sample local cuisine at waterfront cafes, or browse for souvenirs at artisanal craft markets.

Sal's beaches are among the most beautiful in Cape Verde, with soft white sands and crystal-clear waters that stretch for miles along the coastline. Santa Maria Beach, in particular, is a favorite among visitors, with its calm waters and gentle waves perfect for swimming, sunbathing, and water sports such as kiteboarding and windsurfing.

In addition to its beaches, Sal is also known for its natural attractions, including the iconic Salt Pans of Pedra de Lume. This natural saltwater crater, located in the heart of the island, offers visitors the opportunity to float effortlessly in its mineral-rich waters, providing a unique and rejuvenating experience unlike any other.

Sal is also a popular destination for diving and snorkeling, with its clear waters teeming with marine life, colorful coral reefs, and underwater caves waiting to be explored. Dive sites such as Shark Bay and Ponta Preta offer opportunities to encounter a variety of sea creatures, including sea turtles, rays, and tropical fish.

For those seeking adventure on land, Sal offers opportunities for hiking, quad biking, and exploring its dramatic landscapes, including the lunar-like terrain of Pedra de Lume and the rugged cliffs of Ponta do Sino. Visitors can also venture inland to explore the island's quaint villages, salt flats, and volcanic craters, gaining insight into the island's rich history and culture along the way.

With its stunning natural beauty, vibrant culture, and abundance of recreational activities, Sal truly lives up to its reputation as the "Gateway to Cape Verde's Tourism," offering visitors an unforgettable island experience that embodies the spirit of the archipelago.

Mindelo: The Cultural Capital of Cape Verde

Mindelo, known as the "Cultural Capital of Cape Verde," is a vibrant city located on the island of São Vicente, renowned for its rich artistic heritage, lively music scene, and cosmopolitan atmosphere. Situated on a natural harbor overlooking the Atlantic Ocean, Mindelo is a bustling hub of activity, attracting visitors with its colorful colonial architecture, bustling markets, and lively waterfront promenade.

One of the defining features of Mindelo is its thriving music scene, which has earned the city a reputation as the cultural heartbeat of Cape Verde. From traditional genres such as morna and coladeira to contemporary styles like funaná and batuque, music permeates every aspect of life in Mindelo, with live performances, street festivals, and impromptu jam sessions filling the air with rhythm and melody.

The city is also home to a number of cultural institutions and landmarks that showcase Cape Verdean art, history, and heritage. The Centro Cultural do Mindelo, housed in a restored colonial building, hosts exhibitions, concerts, and workshops celebrating the islands' diverse cultural traditions. The Museu do Mar, located on the waterfront, offers insights into Cape Verde's maritime history and fishing heritage, while the

Mercado Municipal provides a colorful glimpse into daily life on the islands, with vendors selling fresh produce, handicrafts, and local delicacies.

In addition to its cultural attractions, Mindelo is known for its lively nightlife, with a plethora of bars, clubs, and live music venues to explore. From cozy jazz cafes to pulsating dance clubs, there's something for everyone to enjoy after dark in Mindelo, with music and dance serving as the lifeblood of the city's social scene.

Mindelo's cultural richness is also reflected in its annual festivals and events, which attract visitors from near and far to celebrate the islands' vibrant traditions and heritage. The annual Baía das Gatas Music Festival, held on the beach outside of Mindelo, showcases Cape Verdean music and culture with performances by local and international artists, while the São Vicente Carnival transforms the streets of Mindelo into a colorful spectacle of costumes, parades, and festivities.

Overall, Mindelo is a city that pulses with creativity, energy, and passion, offering visitors a captivating glimpse into the soul of Cape Verdean culture. Whether exploring its historic streets, savoring its culinary delights, or dancing the night away to the rhythm of its music, Mindelo is a destination that leaves a lasting impression on all who visit.

Praia: Cape Verde's Vibrant Capital City

Praia, Cape Verde's vibrant capital city, is a bustling metropolis located on the southern coast of the island of Santiago. With its rich history, diverse culture, and dynamic atmosphere, Praia serves as the political, economic, and cultural center of the archipelago, attracting visitors with its lively markets, historic landmarks, and thriving arts scene.

Founded in the 16th century, Praia has grown from a small fishing village into a bustling city of over 200,000 residents, making it the largest city in Cape Verde. Its strategic location along major trade routes has made it a hub of commerce and activity, with merchants from Europe, Africa, and the Americas converging on its shores to trade goods and ideas.

One of the highlights of Praia is its historic Old Town, known as Plateau, which is characterized by its cobblestone streets, colonial-era architecture, and picturesque squares. Here, visitors can explore landmarks such as the Presidential Palace, the Cathedral of Our Lady of Grace, and the National Library, which offer insights into the city's colonial past and cultural heritage. Praia is also home to a vibrant arts and cultural scene, with galleries, theaters, and performance spaces showcasing the talents of local artists and

45

musicians. The city's cultural calendar is filled with events such as the Atlantic Music Expo, which brings together artists from across the globe to celebrate Cape Verdean music and culture, and the Festival Internacional de Teatro do Mindelo, which showcases theater productions from around the world. In addition to its cultural attractions, Praia offers visitors a wealth of recreational activities to enjoy, from exploring its sandy beaches and crystalline waters to hiking in the nearby mountains and valleys. The city's coastal promenade, known as Avenida Marginal, is a popular spot for strolling, jogging, and enjoying panoramic views of the ocean.

Praia is also known for its culinary delights, with a diverse array of restaurants, cafes, and eateries serving up traditional Cape Verdean dishes as well as international cuisine. From fresh seafood and grilled meats to tropical fruits and pastries, there's no shortage of flavors to savor in Praia.

Overall, Praia is a city of contrasts and contradictions, where modernity and tradition coexist in harmony, creating a vibrant and dynamic urban landscape that captivates the imagination and leaves a lasting impression on all who visit. Whether exploring its historic streets, immersing oneself in its cultural riches, or simply soaking up the energy of its bustling markets and vibrant neighborhoods, Praia offers a truly unforgettable experience for travelers to Cape Verde.

Santiago: A Historical Perspective

Santiago, the largest and most populous island in Cape Verde, offers a captivating journey through history, culture, and tradition. With its diverse landscapes, rich heritage, and vibrant communities, Santiago is a microcosm of the archipelago's storied past and dynamic present.

The history of Santiago dates back centuries, with evidence of human habitation dating as far back as the 15th century. The island played a central role in the early colonization of Cape Verde by the Portuguese, serving as a strategic outpost for trade and exploration in the Atlantic Ocean.

One of the most significant landmarks on Santiago is the Cidade Velha, or Old Town, a UNESCO World Heritage Site that stands as a testament to the island's colonial past. Founded in the 15th century, Cidade Velha was the first European settlement in the tropics and served as a key port for the transatlantic slave trade, with its historic fortresses, churches, and colonial buildings bearing witness to this dark chapter in history.

In addition to its colonial heritage, Santiago is also home to a rich and diverse cultural tapestry, shaped by centuries of African, European, and indigenous influences. The island's capital city, Praia, is a melting pot of cultures and traditions, with its lively markets, colorful festivals, and vibrant arts scene showcasing the best of Cape Verdean culture.

Santiago's natural beauty is equally captivating, with its rugged mountains, fertile valleys, and golden beaches offering a stunning backdrop for exploration and adventure. The island's interior is characterized by lush vegetation, cascading waterfalls, and picturesque villages, providing ample opportunities for hiking, birdwatching, and eco-tourism.

One of the highlights of Santiago is the Serra Malagueta Natural Park, a protected area that encompasses some of the island's most scenic landscapes, including its highest peak, Pico de Antónia. Here, visitors can explore dense forests, spot rare bird species, and soak in panoramic views of the surrounding countryside.

Santiago's rich history and cultural heritage are also reflected in its culinary traditions, with a diverse array of dishes and flavors to savor. From hearty stews and grilled meats to fresh seafood and tropical fruits, the island's cuisine is a reflection of its multicultural roots, blending African, Portuguese, and indigenous influences into a delicious and distinctive culinary tapestry.

Overall, Santiago offers visitors a fascinating journey through time and culture, with its historic landmarks, vibrant communities, and breathtaking landscapes combining to create an unforgettable island experience. Whether exploring its colonial heritage, immersing oneself in its cultural riches, or simply soaking up the natural beauty of its surroundings, Santiago is a destination that captures the heart and soul of Cape Verde.

São Vicente: Art, Music, and Festivals

São Vicente, an island in the Cape Verde archipelago, is a vibrant hub of art, music, and festivals that pulsates with creativity and cultural energy. Its main city, Mindelo, is often referred to as the cultural capital of Cape Verde, drawing artists, musicians, and visitors from around the world to experience its dynamic atmosphere and rich cultural heritage.

Music is at the heart of São Vicente's identity, with Mindelo serving as a breeding ground for some of Cape Verde's most renowned musicians and musical genres. Morna, the island's most famous musical style, originated in Mindelo and is characterized by its soulful melodies and heartfelt lyrics, often reflecting themes of love, longing, and nostalgia. Cesária Évora, known as the "Barefoot Diva," was born and raised in Mindelo, gaining international acclaim for her mesmerizing voice and soulful renditions of traditional Cape Verdean music.

In addition to morna, São Vicente is also known for its vibrant music scene, with live performances, music festivals, and street parties filling the air with rhythm and melody year-round. The Mindelact Theater Festival, held annually in Mindelo, showcases theater productions from Cape Verde and around the world, while the Baía das Gatas Music Festival, held on the beach outside of Mindelo, attracts thousands of music lovers with its eclectic lineup of local and international artists.

Art is another integral part of São Vicente's cultural landscape, with galleries, studios, and street art adorning the walls of Mindelo's historic buildings. The city's colonial-era architecture serves as a backdrop for artistic expression, with vibrant murals, sculptures, and installations reflecting the island's diverse cultural heritage and creative spirit.

São Vicente is also known for its lively festivals and celebrations, which bring communities together to celebrate their cultural traditions and heritage. The São Vicente Carnival is one of the largest and most colorful festivals in Cape Verde, featuring parades, costumes, and music that transform the streets of Mindelo into a vibrant spectacle of color and creativity. Other popular festivals include the São João Festival, a traditional celebration of Saint John the Baptist, and the Mindelo Cultural Week, which showcases the island's artistic talent through performances, exhibitions, and workshops.

Overall, São Vicente is a vibrant and dynamic island that celebrates its cultural richness and creative spirit with music, art, and festivals that captivate the senses and inspire the soul. Whether exploring its historic streets, immersing oneself in its artistic heritage, or dancing the night away to the rhythm of its music, São Vicente offers visitors an unforgettable experience that embodies the spirit of Cape Verde.

Santo Antão: A Paradise for Hikers

Santo Antão, an island in the Cape Verde archipelago, is a paradise for hikers and nature enthusiasts, offering some of the most breathtaking landscapes and scenic trails in the region. Known for its rugged mountains, verdant valleys, and dramatic coastline, Santo Antão beckons adventurers to explore its diverse terrain and immerse themselves in its natural beauty.

One of the highlights of hiking in Santo Antão is the island's extensive network of trails, which wind their way through mountain passes, lush forests, and remote villages, offering stunning views and unforgettable experiences along the way. The island's diverse landscapes provide a range of hiking options for all levels of experience, from leisurely strolls through scenic valleys to challenging treks up towering peaks.

One of the most popular hiking destinations in Santo Antão is the Cova-Paul-Ribeira da Torre circuit, a multi-day trek that takes hikers through some of the island's most spectacular scenery. Along the way, hikers can explore the lush Paul Valley, with its terraced fields and traditional agricultural practices, and ascend to the rugged peaks of Ribeira da Torre, the highest point on the island, offering panoramic views of the surrounding landscape.

Another must-see hiking destination in Santo Antão is the Ribeira do Paúl Natural Park, a protected area that encompasses some of the island's most pristine and biodiverse ecosystems. Here, hikers can trek through dense forests, cross mountain streams, and encounter a variety of endemic plant and animal species, including the rare Cape Verdean warbler and the elusive chameleon.

Santo Antão is also home to a number of picturesque villages and towns that offer opportunities for cultural immersion and exploration. The village of Ponta do Sol, perched on the edge of a dramatic cliff overlooking the Atlantic Ocean, is a charming destination with its colorful houses, lively markets, and welcoming locals. The village of Fontainhas, known for its terraced fields and stunning views, is another popular stop for hikers looking to experience traditional Cape Verdean life.

In addition to its natural beauty and cultural heritage, Santo Antão is also known for its warm and welcoming hospitality, with guesthouses, eco-lodges, and family-run accommodations offering comfortable and authentic experiences for travelers. Whether exploring its scenic trails, immersing oneself in its vibrant culture, or simply relaxing and enjoying the island's natural beauty, Santo Antão offers a truly unforgettable experience for hikers and adventurers alike.

Boa Vista: Dunes, Turtles, and More

Boa Vista, one of the islands in the Cape Verde archipelago, is a treasure trove of natural wonders, with its expansive sand dunes, pristine beaches, and diverse wildlife attracting visitors from around the world. Located in the eastern part of the archipelago, Boa Vista is renowned for its stunning landscapes and rich biodiversity, offering a wide range of experiences for nature lovers and outdoor enthusiasts.

The island's most iconic feature is its vast desert-like landscape, characterized by towering sand dunes that stretch as far as the eye can see. The dunes of Boa Vista are a sight to behold, with their golden sands shifting and changing shape with the wind, creating an ever-changing landscape that is both awe-inspiring and mesmerizing.

In addition to its dunes, Boa Vista is also home to some of the most beautiful beaches in Cape Verde, with pristine white sands and crystal-clear waters that beckon visitors to relax, swim, and soak up the sun. The beaches of Boa Vista, such as Santa Monica Beach and Chaves Beach, are also important nesting grounds for endangered sea turtles, including loggerheads and hawksbills, which come ashore to lay their eggs during the nesting season.

Boa Vista's beaches are not only important for sea turtles but also for a variety of other marine life, including colorful fish, dolphins, and whales. Snorkeling and diving are popular activities in Boa Vista, offering visitors the chance to explore vibrant coral reefs, underwater caves, and shipwrecks teeming with life.

In addition to its natural beauty, Boa Vista is also known for its vibrant culture and warm hospitality, with traditional Cape Verdean music, dance, and cuisine adding to the island's charm. Visitors to Boa Vista can sample local dishes such as cachupa, a hearty stew made with corn, beans, and vegetables, or listen to live music at one of the island's many bars and restaurants.

Overall, Boa Vista offers visitors a unique and unforgettable experience, with its stunning landscapes, abundant wildlife, and rich cultural heritage combining to create a destination that is truly one-of-a-kind. Whether exploring its dunes, swimming in its crystal-clear waters, or immersing oneself in its vibrant culture, Boa Vista is a place that leaves a lasting impression on all who visit.

Fogo: The Volcanic Heart of Cape Verde

Fogo, aptly named for its fiery volcanic landscapes, is truly the volcanic heart of Cape Verde. This captivating island is dominated by one of the most iconic natural landmarks in the archipelago: Pico do Fogo, an active volcano that towers over the island's landscape. Pico do Fogo stands at an impressive 2,829 meters (9,281 feet) above sea level, making it the highest peak in Cape Verde and a magnet for adventurers and nature enthusiasts alike.

The volcanic activity on Fogo has shaped the island's terrain and influenced its culture and way of life. The island's fertile soils, enriched by volcanic ash and lava, support lush vegetation and thriving agriculture, making Fogo one of the most productive agricultural regions in Cape Verde. The island is known for its vineyards, which produce the renowned Fogo wine, as well as its coffee plantations, orchards, and vegetable gardens.

The town of São Filipe, nestled at the base of Pico do Fogo, serves as the gateway to the volcano and the cultural capital of the island. With its charming colonial architecture, colorful markets, and vibrant cultural scene, São Filipe offers visitors a glimpse into the island's rich history and heritage. The town is also home to a number of artisanal workshops and galleries, where visitors can purchase locally-made crafts and souvenirs. For adventurers seeking to explore Pico do Fogo and its otherworldly landscapes, guided hikes to the summit of the volcano are a must. The hike to the summit is challenging but rewarding, offering breathtaking views of the island and its surrounding seascape. Along the way, hikers can witness the dramatic changes in vegetation as they ascend from lush forests to barren volcanic slopes, and marvel at the volcanic craters, lava fields, and steam vents that dot the landscape.

In addition to its volcanic landscapes, Fogo is also known for its vibrant culture and traditions, which are deeply rooted in the island's African and Portuguese heritage. Traditional music, dance, and festivals play an important role in the island's cultural identity, with events such as the São Filipe Carnival and the Festival de Música da Praia exemplifying the island's lively spirit and creative energy.

Overall, Fogo is a destination that captivates the imagination and ignites the senses, with its dramatic volcanic landscapes, rich cultural heritage, and warm hospitality leaving a lasting impression on all who visit. Whether exploring the slopes of Pico do Fogo, savoring the flavors of Fogo wine, or dancing to the rhythm of Cape Verdean music, Fogo offers a truly unforgettable experience for travelers seeking adventure, culture, and natural beauty.

Brava: The Island of Flowers

Brava, known as the "Island of Flowers," is a hidden gem in the Cape Verde archipelago, celebrated for its lush landscapes, colorful blooms, and tranquil atmosphere. Situated in the southern part of the archipelago, Brava is the smallest and least populated island in Cape Verde, offering visitors a serene retreat from the hustle and bustle of everyday life.

One of the defining features of Brava is its verdant valleys and fertile plains, which are crisscrossed by meandering streams and dotted with vibrant flowers and vegetation. The island's temperate climate and abundant rainfall create ideal conditions for plant life to thrive, resulting in a rich tapestry of colors and fragrances that delight the senses year-round.

The town of Nova Sintra, nestled in the heart of Brava, serves as the island's main hub and cultural center. With its charming colonial architecture, picturesque squares, and scenic vistas, Nova Sintra offers visitors a glimpse into the island's rich history and heritage. The town is also home to a number of artisanal workshops and boutiques, where visitors can purchase locally-made crafts and souvenirs.

In addition to its natural beauty, Brava is also known for its warm and welcoming hospitality, with a strong sense of community and tradition that permeates every aspect of life on the island. Visitors to Brava can experience traditional Cape Verdean culture firsthand through music, dance, and local festivals, which celebrate the island's unique identity and heritage.

One of the highlights of visiting Brava is exploring its scenic coastline and pristine beaches, which offer opportunities for swimming, snorkeling, and relaxation in a tranquil setting. The island's rugged cliffs and rocky coves provide stunning views of the Atlantic Ocean, while its secluded bays and inlets offer secluded spots for picnics and sunbathing.

For outdoor enthusiasts, Brava also offers a variety of hiking trails that wind through its lush interior, offering panoramic views of the surrounding landscape and opportunities to spot native wildlife such as birds, lizards, and butterflies. The island's highest peak, Monte Fontainhas, offers a challenging but rewarding hike with breathtaking views of the island and its neighboring islets.

Overall, Brava is a destination that captivates the senses and soothes the soul, with its stunning natural beauty, warm hospitality, and tranquil atmosphere creating an idyllic retreat for travelers seeking peace and serenity. Whether exploring its flower-filled valleys, relaxing on its pristine beaches, or immersing oneself in its rich cultural heritage, Brava offers a truly unforgettable experience for those who venture to its shores.

São Nicolau: A Haven for Nature Lovers

São Nicolau, nestled in the Cape Verde archipelago, stands out as a haven for nature lovers, offering a diverse array of landscapes and ecosystems to explore. This charming island, located between São Vicente and Sal, boasts rugged mountains, verdant valleys, and picturesque beaches, making it a paradise for outdoor enthusiasts seeking adventure and tranquility.

One of the highlights of São Nicolau is its dramatic mountain ranges, which dominate the island's interior and offer countless opportunities for hiking, trekking, and exploration. The island's highest peak, Monte Gordo, rises to an impressive 1,312 meters (4,304 feet) above sea level, offering panoramic views of the surrounding landscape and the neighboring islands. Hiking trails crisscross the mountains, leading visitors through lush forests, past cascading waterfalls, and into hidden valleys teeming with life.

In addition to its mountains, São Nicolau is also known for its fertile valleys and agricultural landscapes, which support a variety of crops including coffee, sugarcane, and fruits. The valleys of Ribeira Brava and Ribeira da Prata are particularly scenic, with terraced fields cascading down the slopes and traditional villages nestled among the greenery. Visitors to São Nicolau can explore these valleys on foot or by car, stopping to admire the views and sample locally-grown produce along the way.

São Nicolau's coastline is equally captivating, with rugged cliffs, secluded coves, and pristine beaches that offer opportunities for swimming, snorkeling, and relaxation. The beach at Tarrafal de São Nicolau is one of the island's most popular spots, with its golden sands and turquoise waters providing a tranquil setting for sunbathing and water sports.

For birdwatchers and nature enthusiasts, São Nicolau offers a wealth of opportunities to observe native wildlife in its natural habitat. The island is home to a variety of bird species, including the endemic Cape Verde warbler and the endangered Cape Verde shearwater, as well as reptiles, amphibians, and marine life.

In addition to its natural beauty, São Nicolau is also known for its warm hospitality and rich cultural heritage, with traditional music, dance, and festivals playing an important role in island life. Visitors to São Nicolau can experience Cape Verdean culture firsthand through local events such as the Festival de São João, a traditional celebration of Saint John the Baptist, and the Festa da Praia, a lively beach festival held in August.

Overall, São Nicolau is a destination that appeals to nature lovers, adventure seekers, and culture enthusiasts alike, with its stunning landscapes, diverse ecosystems, and vibrant culture offering a truly unforgettable experience for those who venture to its shores. Whether hiking in the mountains, relaxing on the beach, or immersing oneself in island life, São Nicolau is a hidden gem waiting to be discovered.

Maio: Tranquility and Seclusion

Maio, a serene and secluded island in the Cape Verde archipelago, beckons travelers seeking tranquility and escape from the hustle and bustle of modern life. Situated between Santiago and Boa Vista, Maio is characterized by its pristine beaches, sleepy villages, and laid-back atmosphere, making it the perfect destination for those looking to unwind and reconnect with nature.

One of the defining features of Maio is its stunning coastline, which stretches for miles and boasts some of the most beautiful beaches in Cape Verde. From the powdery white sands of Morro Beach to the crystal-clear waters of Santana Beach, Maio's beaches offer endless opportunities for swimming, sunbathing, and relaxation in a tranquil setting. The island's remote location and lack of crowds make it a peaceful retreat for beachgoers looking to escape the crowds and immerse themselves in nature.

In addition to its beaches, Maio is also known for its diverse landscapes, which range from rolling sand dunes to verdant valleys and rocky cliffs. The interior of the island is sparsely populated, with vast stretches of undeveloped land that offer opportunities for hiking, birdwatching, and wildlife spotting. The island's diverse ecosystems support a variety of plant and animal species, including rare birds such as the Cape Verde kite and the Raso lark.

The main town on Maio is Vila do Maio, a charming fishing village that serves as the island's administrative center and cultural hub. With its colorful houses, cobblestone streets, and bustling markets, Vila do Maio offers visitors a glimpse into the island's rich history and heritage. The town is also home to a number of restaurants, cafes, and bars where visitors can sample local cuisine and mingle with the friendly locals.

For outdoor enthusiasts, Maio offers a range of activities to enjoy, from windsurfing and kiteboarding to fishing and sailing. The island's warm waters and steady trade winds make it an ideal destination for water sports, while its unspoiled landscapes provide a peaceful backdrop for hiking, biking, and exploring.

Overall, Maio is a destination that captivates the imagination and soothes the soul, with its tranquil beaches, diverse landscapes, and laid-back atmosphere offering a welcome respite from the stresses of everyday life. Whether lounging on the beach, exploring the island's natural beauty, or immersing oneself in its rich culture, Maio is a hidden gem waiting to be discovered by travelers seeking serenity and seclusion.

Historic Landmarks: Exploring Cape Verde's Architectural Treasures

Cape Verde's rich history is reflected in its architectural treasures, which span centuries and showcase a blend of influences from Africa, Europe, and beyond. Exploring the historic landmarks of Cape Verde offers a fascinating journey through time, with each building and monument telling a story of the island's past and cultural heritage.

One of the most iconic landmarks in Cape Verde is Cidade Velha, the oldest settlement in the archipelago and a UNESCO World Heritage Site. Founded in the 15th century, Cidade Velha served as a strategic trading post and hub for Portuguese explorers during the Age of Discovery. Today, visitors to Cidade Velha can explore its historic streets, colonial-era buildings, and imposing fortresses, including the Fortaleza Real de São Filipe, which overlooks the town and offers panoramic views of the Atlantic Ocean.

Another architectural gem in Cape Verde is the Palácio do Povo, located in the capital city of Praia on the island of Santiago. Built in the early 20th century, the Palácio do Povo is a striking example of colonial architecture, with its grand facade, ornate detailing, and spacious interior reflecting the island's colonial past and Portuguese heritage. Today, the Palácio do Povo serves as the seat of government and a venue for cultural events and exhibitions.

In addition to its colonial-era buildings, Cape Verde is also home to a number of historic churches and cathedrals that showcase the island's religious heritage and architectural prowess. One notable example is the Sé Cathedral in Mindelo, São Vicente, a majestic neo-Gothic structure that dominates the city's skyline and serves as a symbol of faith and community.

Throughout Cape Verde, visitors will also find a wealth of traditional Cape Verdean architecture, characterized by its colorful facades, tiled roofs, and intricate wooden balconies. The town of Ribeira Grande on the island of Santo Antão is known for its well-preserved colonial architecture, with its historic buildings and cobblestone streets providing a glimpse into the island's past as a prosperous trading center.

Overall, exploring Cape Verde's architectural treasures offers a fascinating glimpse into the island's history, culture, and heritage. Whether wandering through the historic streets of Cidade Velha, admiring the grandeur of the Palácio do Povo, or marveling at the craftsmanship of traditional Cape Verdean homes, visitors to Cape Verde are sure to be captivated by the island's rich architectural legacy.

Maritime Legacy: Cape Verde's Nautical Heritage

Cape Verde's nautical heritage is deeply intertwined with its history and culture, shaped by centuries of seafaring traditions and maritime exploration. Situated in the Atlantic Ocean off the coast of West Africa, the islands of Cape Verde have long been a strategic stopover for sailors, traders, and explorers navigating the waters between Europe, Africa, and the Americas.

One of the defining features of Cape Verde's maritime legacy is its role as a key waypoint on the transatlantic slave trade route. From the 15th to the 19th centuries, Cape Verde served as a crucial hub for the transportation of enslaved Africans to the New World, with ships departing from its ports laden with human cargo bound for plantations in the Americas. Today, the legacy of the transatlantic slave trade is commemorated through museums, monuments, and cultural initiatives that seek to honor the memory of those who suffered and perished.

In addition to its role in the slave trade, Cape Verde has a rich history of maritime exploration and adventure. Portuguese explorers, including Diogo Gomes and António da Noli, are credited with the discovery and colonization of the islands in the 15th century, paving the way for centuries of Portuguese influence and settlement. The islands' strategic location made them an important base for expeditions to the New World, with ships stopping in Cape Verde to resupply and refuel before embarking on their transatlantic voyages. Throughout its history, Cape Verde has been home to a vibrant maritime culture, with fishing playing a central role in the livelihoods of many islanders. Traditional fishing techniques, such as handline fishing and seine netting, are still practiced today, providing a sustainable source of food and income for coastal communities. In addition to fishing, Cape Verdean sailors are renowned for their skills in navigating the treacherous waters of the Atlantic Ocean, with many islanders serving as crew members on international shipping vessels and cruise ships. Today, Cape Verde's maritime heritage is celebrated through festivals, regattas, and cultural events that pay homage to the island's seafaring traditions. The Mindelo International Maritime Music Festival, held annually in São Vicente, showcases the rich musical and maritime heritage of Cape Verde, with performances by local and international artists and sailing competitions that attract sailors from around the world.

Overall, Cape Verde's nautical heritage is a testament to the island's resilience, ingenuity, and spirit of adventure. From its role in the transatlantic slave trade to its tradition of maritime exploration and fishing, Cape Verde's maritime legacy continues to shape the identity and culture of the islands to this day.

Cape Verdean Festivals: Celebrating Life and Culture

Cape Verdean festivals are vibrant celebrations of life, culture, and tradition that bring communities together in joyous revelry. Throughout the year, the islands come alive with music, dance, and colorful parades that showcase the rich cultural heritage of Cape Verde.

One of the most iconic festivals in Cape Verde is Carnival, a lively and exuberant celebration that takes place in the weeks leading up to Lent. Carnival is celebrated with fervor on many of the islands, with each island putting its own unique spin on the festivities. In Mindelo, São Vicente, Carnival is known for its elaborate costumes, samba music, and street parades that draw crowds of locals and visitors alike. In Praia, Santiago, Carnival takes on a more traditional flavor, with colorful processions, masquerade balls, and cultural performances that pay homage to the island's African and Portuguese heritage.

Another highlight of the Cape Verdean festival calendar is the Festival de Música da Praia, held annually in Praia, Santiago. This vibrant music festival showcases the best in Cape Verdean music, with performances by local and international artists spanning genres such as morna, coladeira, and funaná. The festival attracts music lovers from across the archipelago and beyond, providing a platform for emerging talent and established stars to shine.

In addition to music festivals, Cape Verde is also home to a number of religious and cultural celebrations that reflect the island's diverse heritage and traditions. The Festival of São João, celebrated in June, is a colorful and lively festival that honors Saint John the Baptist with feasting, dancing, and bonfires. The Festival of Santa Catarina, held in November on the island of Santiago, is a religious celebration that combines Catholic rituals with traditional Cape Verdean music and dance.

Throughout the year, Cape Verdeans also celebrate various saints' days, harvest festivals, and cultural events that highlight the island's culinary traditions, folklore, and craftsmanship. These festivals are often accompanied by traditional dishes such as cachupa, a hearty stew made with corn, beans, and meat, and grogue, a strong spirit made from sugarcane.

Overall, Cape Verdean festivals are a testament to the island's vibrant culture, spirit of community, and zest for life. Whether celebrating Carnival in the streets of Mindelo, dancing to the rhythm of morna in Praia, or honoring saints and traditions in villages across the archipelago, Cape Verdeans know how to throw a party that is sure to leave a lasting impression on all who participate.

Legends and Folklore: Stories from Cape Verde

Legends and folklore weave a rich tapestry of storytelling and tradition in Cape Verde, offering insight into the island's cultural heritage and collective imagination. Passed down through generations, these stories are a reflection of the islanders' beliefs, values, and worldview, providing a window into the soul of Cape Verde.

One of the most famous legends in Cape Verdean folklore is the story of A Nha Cretcheu, or "My Beloved." This tale tells of a young woman who falls in love with a sailor and waits faithfully for his return, only to be tragically abandoned when he fails to come back. A Nha Cretcheu is often depicted as a symbol of love, longing, and the transient nature of life on the islands.

Another popular legend is that of the Pedra de Lume, a salt lake on the island of Sal that is said to be haunted by the spirits of slaves who toiled in the salt mines centuries ago. According to legend, the ghostly figures of slaves can be seen at night, wandering the shores of the lake and lamenting their tragic fate. The Pedra de Lume is now a popular tourist attraction, with visitors drawn to its eerie beauty and haunting history.

Cape Verdean folklore is also rich in stories of supernatural beings and mythical creatures. One such creature is the Morna, a mischievous spirit that is said to inhabit the mountains and forests of the islands. According to legend, the Morna can take on various forms, from a beautiful woman to a fearsome beast, and is known for playing tricks on unsuspecting travelers.

In addition to legends and folklore, Cape Verdean culture is also steeped in superstition and belief in the supernatural. Many islanders still adhere to traditional practices such as witchcraft, divination, and ancestor worship, seeking guidance and protection from the spirits that inhabit the natural world.

Overall, legends and folklore play a central role in Cape Verdean culture, shaping the way islanders view the world and their place in it. Whether recounting tales of love and loss, exploring the mysteries of the supernatural, or seeking solace in the wisdom of their ancestors, the stories of Cape Verde are as diverse and captivating as the islands themselves.

The Cape Verdean Diaspora: Spreading Culture Across the Globe

The Cape Verdean diaspora is a global phenomenon that has seen millions of Cape Verdeans spread out across the world, taking their culture, traditions, and values with them wherever they go. From the shores of West Africa to the streets of New England, the Cape Verdean diaspora is a testament to the resilience and adaptability of the Cape Verdean people in the face of adversity.

One of the largest Cape Verdean diaspora communities can be found in the United States, particularly in cities like Boston, Providence, and New Bedford, Massachusetts. These communities trace their roots back to the 19th century, when Cape Verdeans began immigrating to the United States in search of economic opportunity and a better life. Today, the Cape Verdean diaspora in the United States is thriving, with vibrant communities that celebrate Cape Verdean culture through music, dance, food, and festivals.

In addition to the United States, Cape Verdean communities can be found in countries around the world, including Portugal, the Netherlands,

France, and Brazil. These diaspora communities have played a vital role in preserving and promoting Cape Verdean culture and identity, serving as cultural ambassadors and advocates for the islands on the global stage.

One of the most visible expressions of Cape Verdean culture in the diaspora is through music, particularly genres such as morna, coladeira, and funaná. Cape Verdean musicians and artists have achieved international acclaim, with performers like Cesária Évora, Tito Paris, and Mayra Andrade gaining recognition for their talent and artistry. Their music serves as a bridge between the islands and the wider world, bringing Cape Verdean culture to audiences around the globe.

In addition to music, Cape Verdean cuisine has also made its mark on the diaspora, with dishes like cachupa, pastéis de bacalhau, and grogue becoming beloved staples in Cape Verdean communities worldwide. Restaurants, cafes, and food festivals offer opportunities for Cape Verdeans and non-Cape Verdeans alike to experience the flavors and culinary traditions of the islands.

Overall, the Cape Verdean diaspora is a testament to the enduring spirit and cultural richness of the Cape Verdean people. Despite being scattered across the globe, Cape Verdeans remain deeply connected to their roots, carrying with them the traditions, values, and spirit of Cape Verde wherever they go. Through their contributions to music, food, art, and more, the Cape Verdean diaspora continues to spread the vibrant culture of the islands to every corner of the earth.

Sustainable Tourism: Preserving Cape Verde's Beauty

Sustainable tourism is crucial for preserving the natural beauty and cultural heritage of Cape Verde, ensuring that future generations can continue to enjoy the islands' unique charm and resources. With its stunning beaches, diverse landscapes, and rich cultural traditions, Cape Verde has become an increasingly popular destination for travelers seeking adventure, relaxation, and cultural immersion.

However, the rapid growth of tourism in recent years has also brought challenges such as overdevelopment, environmental degradation, and cultural erosion. To address these issues, Cape Verde has implemented various measures to promote sustainable tourism practices and minimize the negative impacts of tourism on the islands' ecosystems and communities.

One of the key principles of sustainable tourism in Cape Verde is environmental conservation. The islands are home to a wide variety of ecosystems, including coastal dunes, volcanic landscapes, and marine habitats, which are vulnerable to damage from tourism-related activities such as construction, pollution, and overfishing. To protect these fragile ecosystems, Cape Verde has established national parks, marine reserves, and protected areas where tourism is carefully managed to minimize its impact on the environment.

In addition to environmental conservation, sustainable tourism in Cape Verde also focuses on promoting cultural preservation and community empowerment. The islands have a rich cultural heritage, with traditions, languages, and customs that date back centuries. By supporting local artisans, musicians, and cultural events, tourism can help to preserve these traditions and generate income for local communities.

Community-based tourism initiatives, such as homestays, guided tours, and cultural exchanges, provide opportunities for travelers to engage directly with Cape Verdean communities, learn about their way of life, and contribute to local economies in a sustainable and responsible manner. By fostering meaningful connections between tourists and locals, community-based tourism helps to promote cross-cultural understanding and mutual respect, enriching the travel experience for both parties.

Another aspect of sustainable tourism in Cape Verde is the promotion of responsible travel practices among visitors. This includes respecting local customs and traditions, minimizing waste and pollution, and supporting businesses that prioritize sustainability and social responsibility. By making informed choices about where to stay, what to eat, and how to get around, travelers can reduce their environmental footprint and contribute positively to the local economy and community.

Overall, sustainable tourism is essential for preserving Cape Verde's beauty and ensuring the long-term viability of its tourism industry. By balancing the needs of the environment, the economy, and the community, Cape Verde can continue to thrive as a world-class destination for travelers while safeguarding its natural and cultural heritage for future generations to enjoy.

Governance and Politics: Understanding Cape Verde's System

Understanding Cape Verde's governance and political system provides insight into the country's history, development, and democratic values. Since gaining independence from Portugal in 1975, Cape Verde has established itself as one of Africa's most stable and democratic nations, with a multi-party political system, regular elections, and a commitment to good governance.

At the heart of Cape Verde's political system is the Constitution, which guarantees fundamental rights and freedoms, establishes the separation of powers, and outlines the structure and functions of the government. The Constitution also enshrines principles such as the rule of law, accountability, and transparency, which form the foundation of Cape Verde's democratic governance.

Cape Verde operates under a semi-presidential system of government, with power divided between the President, who serves as the head of state, and the Prime Minister, who serves as the head of government. The President is elected by popular vote for a maximum of two five-year terms and has powers that include appointing the Prime Minister, vetoing legislation, and representing Cape Verde on the international stage. The Prime Minister is appointed by the President and is responsible for leading the government and implementing its policies.

The legislative branch of government in Cape Verde is comprised of the National Assembly, a unicameral parliament with 72 members elected by proportional representation for four-year terms. The National Assembly is responsible for enacting legislation, overseeing the executive branch, and representing the interests of the people. It plays a vital role in shaping the country's laws, policies, and priorities through debate, negotiation, and consensus-building.

Cape Verde's political landscape is characterized by a multi-party system, with several political parties competing for power and representation in government. The two main political parties are the African Party for the Independence of Cape Verde (PAICV) and the Movement for Democracy (MpD), which have historically alternated in power through free and fair elections. Other smaller parties also play a role in Cape Verdean politics, representing a diverse range of ideologies and interests.

Despite its small size and limited resources, Cape Verde has earned a reputation as a model of good governance and political stability in Africa. The country consistently ranks highly on global indices of democracy, transparency, and human development, reflecting its commitment to democratic values, the rule of law, and inclusive development.

Overall, understanding Cape Verde's governance and political system is essential for grasping the country's journey from colonialism to independence and its ongoing efforts to build a prosperous and democratic society for all its citizens. By embracing democratic principles, fostering political participation, and upholding the rule of law, Cape Verde continues to chart a course toward a brighter future for itself and its people.

Education and Healthcare: Progress and Challenges

Education and healthcare are two pillars of social development in Cape Verde, reflecting the government's commitment to improving the well-being and quality of life of its citizens. Since gaining independence in 1975, Cape Verde has made significant strides in expanding access to education and healthcare services, but challenges remain in ensuring equity, quality, and sustainability across these sectors.

In terms of education, Cape Verde has made impressive progress in increasing enrollment rates and expanding access to schooling at all levels. The government has implemented policies aimed at promoting universal access to education, with initiatives such as the National Education Plan and the Education for All program, which seek to improve the quality of education, reduce dropout rates, and enhance teacher training and professional development.

As a result of these efforts, primary school enrollment rates in Cape Verde are among the highest in Africa, with nearly universal enrollment at the primary level. However, challenges persist in ensuring access to quality education for all children, particularly those living in rural and remote areas, where infrastructure and resources may be limited. Additionally, disparities in educational outcomes persist between urban and rural areas, as well as between boys and girls, highlighting the need for targeted interventions to address these inequalities.

In the healthcare sector, Cape Verde has also made significant progress in expanding access to essential healthcare services and improving health outcomes for its population. The government has invested in the development of healthcare infrastructure, including hospitals, clinics, and health centers, to ensure that all citizens have access to basic healthcare services, regardless of their location or socioeconomic status.

Cape Verde has also implemented policies aimed at improving public health outcomes, such as the National Health Plan and the Expanded Program on Immunization, which seek to prevent and control communicable diseases, reduce maternal and child mortality rates, and promote healthy behaviors and lifestyles. As a result, Cape Verde has seen notable improvements in health indicators such as life expectancy, infant mortality, and maternal mortality, with rates comparable to those of more developed countries.

Despite these achievements, challenges remain in the healthcare sector, particularly in addressing the burden of noncommunicable diseases such as diabetes, hypertension, and cardiovascular disease, which are on the rise due to changing lifestyles and dietary habits. Additionally, access to specialized healthcare services, such as mental health care and treatment for chronic diseases, remains limited, particularly in rural areas.

Overall, education and healthcare are critical components of Cape Verde's development agenda, with progress made in expanding access to these essential services for all citizens. However, challenges remain in ensuring equity, quality, and sustainability in these sectors, requiring continued investment, innovation, and collaboration between government, civil society, and the private sector to address these challenges and build a healthier, more educated society for future generations.

Economic Development: Industries and Growth Sectors

Economic development is a cornerstone of Cape Verde's progress and prosperity, with the government and private sector working hand in hand to diversify the economy, create jobs, and improve the standard of living for its citizens. Since gaining independence in 1975, Cape Verde has transitioned from a predominantly agrarian economy to a more diversified economy with a focus on tourism, services, and renewable energy.

Tourism is one of the main drivers of economic growth in Cape Verde, with the sector contributing significantly to GDP and employment. The islands' natural beauty, pristine beaches, and vibrant culture attract visitors from around the world, providing opportunities for investment, job creation, and revenue generation. The government has invested in tourism infrastructure, including hotels, resorts, and airports, to support the industry's growth and enhance the visitor experience.

In addition to tourism, Cape Verde has also developed other key industries such as fisheries, agriculture, and renewable energy. The fishing industry plays a vital role in the economy, providing employment and income for thousands of Cape Verdeans engaged in fishing, processing, and exporting fish and seafood products. The government has implemented policies to promote sustainable fishing practices and ensure the long-term viability of the industry.

Agriculture remains an important sector of the economy, despite its relatively small contribution to GDP. The islands' arid climate and limited arable land present challenges for agricultural production, but Cape Verde has made strides in improving productivity and sustainability through investments in irrigation, soil conservation, and crop diversification. Key agricultural products include fruits, vegetables, and cash crops such as sugarcane and bananas.

Renewable energy is another area of focus for economic development in Cape Verde, given the islands' abundant natural resources such as wind, solar, and water. The government has invested in renewable energy infrastructure, including wind farms, solar power plants, and hydroelectric projects, to reduce dependence on imported fossil fuels and promote energy independence. Cape Verde aims to generate 100% of its electricity from renewable sources by 2025, positioning the islands as a leader in sustainable energy development in Africa.

Overall, economic development in Cape Verde is characterized by diversification, innovation, and resilience, with the government and private sector working together to harness the islands' natural and human resources for sustainable growth and prosperity. While challenges such as limited natural resources, geographic isolation, and vulnerability to external shocks persist, Cape Verde is well-positioned to overcome these challenges and build a brighter future for its citizens through continued investment, innovation, and strategic planning.

Climate Change and Environmental Sustainability

Climate change and environmental sustainability are pressing issues for Cape Verde, a country vulnerable to the impacts of rising temperatures, changing weather patterns, and sea-level rise. Located in the Atlantic Ocean off the coast of West Africa, Cape Verde is particularly susceptible to the effects of climate change due to its small size, limited natural resources, and dependence on agriculture, fisheries, and tourism.

One of the most significant impacts of climate change on Cape Verde is the increase in temperatures and changes in rainfall patterns, leading to more frequent and severe droughts, heatwaves, and water scarcity. These changes pose significant challenges for agriculture, which employs a large portion of the population and relies heavily on rainfall for irrigation and crop production. Drought-resistant crops, water conservation measures, and sustainable land management practices are essential for adapting to these challenges and ensuring food security for Cape Verde's population.

Rising sea levels and coastal erosion are also major concerns for Cape Verde, threatening infrastructure, livelihoods, and ecosystems along the coastline. The islands' sandy beaches, coral reefs, and mangrove forests provide essential protection against erosion and storm surges, but they are increasingly vulnerable to degradation due to climate change and human activities such as coastal development, sand mining, and overfishing. Coastal protection measures, such as beach nourishment, mangrove restoration, and the construction of sea walls, are critical for safeguarding the islands' coastline and mitigating the impacts of sea-level rise.

In addition to the direct impacts of climate change, Cape Verde also faces challenges related to environmental sustainability, including deforestation, soil erosion, pollution, and waste management. Rapid population growth, urbanization, and economic development have put pressure on the islands' natural resources, leading to habitat loss, biodiversity decline, and degradation of ecosystems. Sustainable land use planning, reforestation efforts, waste reduction initiatives, and renewable energy development are essential for promoting environmental sustainability and mitigating the impacts of climate change.

Despite these challenges, Cape Verde has taken steps to address climate change and promote environmental sustainability through policy initiatives, international partnerships, and community-based conservation efforts. The government has developed national strategies and action plans for climate change adaptation and mitigation, including the National Adaptation Plan and the National Climate Change Policy, which aim to mainstream climate considerations into development planning and decision-making processes.

International cooperation and support are also critical for Cape Verde's efforts to address climate change and promote environmental sustainability. The country is a signatory to international agreements such as the Paris Agreement and the United Nations Framework Convention on Climate Change, which commit Cape Verde to reducing greenhouse gas emissions, enhancing resilience to climate impacts, and mobilizing financial and technical support for adaptation and mitigation efforts.

Overall, climate change and environmental sustainability are complex and interconnected challenges that require concerted action at the local, national, and global levels. By investing in adaptation measures, promoting sustainable development practices, and strengthening resilience to climate impacts, Cape Verde can build a more resilient and sustainable future for its people and its environment.

Religion and Spirituality: Faith in Cape Verde

Religion and spirituality hold significant importance in the cultural fabric of Cape Verde, shaping the beliefs, traditions, and values of its people. The islands are home to a diverse array of religious practices, reflecting the influences of African, European, and indigenous cultures that have shaped Cape Verdean society over the centuries.

Christianity is the dominant religion in Cape Verde, with the Catholic Church being the largest Christian denomination. The majority of Cape Verdeans are Roman Catholic, with Catholicism playing a central role in daily life, community events, and cultural celebrations. Churches, cathedrals, and religious festivals are prominent features of Cape Verdean society, providing opportunities for worship, fellowship, and spiritual growth.

In addition to Catholicism, Protestantism has also gained a foothold in Cape Verde, with various Protestant denominations such as Baptists, Methodists, and Pentecostals present on the islands. Protestant churches and evangelical movements have attracted followers with their emphasis on personal faith, biblical teachings, and charismatic worship styles, appealing to Cape Verdeans seeking alternative expressions of

Christianity. Alongside Christianity, Islam has a significant presence in Cape Verde, particularly among the immigrant communities from West Africa and North Africa. Mosques and Islamic centers can be found in major cities and towns, serving the spiritual needs of Muslim residents and visitors. Islam coexists peacefully with other religions in Cape Verde, reflecting the country's tradition of religious tolerance and pluralism.

In addition to these mainstream religions, Cape Verde is also home to indigenous spiritual beliefs and practices rooted in African traditions. Animism, ancestor worship, and spiritual healing are integral aspects of Cape Verdean culture, with rituals, ceremonies, and oral traditions passed down through generations. These indigenous beliefs often intersect with Christianity and Islam, creating syncretic forms of spirituality unique to Cape Verde.

Overall, religion and spirituality play a central role in the lives of Cape Verdeans, providing a source of comfort, guidance, and community cohesion. Despite the diversity of religious practices, Cape Verdeans share a common respect for religious freedom, tolerance, and mutual understanding, fostering a spirit of unity and cooperation across different faith traditions. Religion continues to shape the cultural identity and social fabric of Cape Verde, enriching the lives of its people and contributing to the country's vibrant and diverse heritage.

Family and Community: Social Fabric of Cape Verde

Family and community are the bedrock of Cape Verdean society, forming the intricate social fabric that binds together its people in shared values, traditions, and support networks. In Cape Verde, family extends beyond blood relations to encompass close-knit communities and networks of friends, neighbors, and acquaintances who provide mutual aid, solidarity, and emotional support in times of need.

The concept of family in Cape Verde is broad and inclusive, encompassing not only immediate relatives but also extended family members, godparents, and honorary kinship ties. Family ties are deeply rooted in Cape Verdean culture, with strong bonds of kinship, loyalty, and reciprocity that transcend geographical distance and generational divides. Families often gather for celebrations, holidays, and special occasions, reinforcing bonds of love, connection, and shared identity.

Community plays a central role in Cape Verdean life, with neighborhoods, villages, and towns serving as hubs of social interaction, cooperation, and collective action. Communities in Cape Verde are characterized by a sense of belonging, cooperation, and solidarity, with residents coming together to address common challenges, celebrate achievements, and preserve cultural traditions. Mutual aid associations, neighborhood committees, and cultural organizations play important roles in fostering community cohesion and resilience.

In Cape Verdean culture, respect for elders and authority figures is deeply ingrained, with elders serving as repositories of wisdom, knowledge, and experience. Elders are revered for their role in preserving cultural heritage, passing down oral traditions, and imparting life lessons to younger generations. The concept of "família" extends beyond the nuclear family to include the broader community, with individuals often referring to close friends and acquaintances as "familia" as a sign of affection and solidarity.

Gender roles and expectations also play a significant role in Cape Verdean family and community life, with women traditionally assuming primary responsibility for domestic duties and childcare while men are often regarded as providers and protectors of the family. However, these roles are evolving as Cape Verdean society modernizes, with increasing opportunities for women in education, employment, and leadership roles.

Overall, family and community are integral to the social fabric of Cape Verde, providing a sense of identity, belonging, and interconnectedness that shapes the lives of its people. Through strong family bonds, vibrant community networks, and shared cultural values, Cape Verdeans find strength, resilience, and support in the face of adversity, fostering a sense of unity and solidarity that transcends individual differences and unites them as a people.

Traditional Crafts and Artisans

In Cape Verde, traditional crafts and artisanal skills are deeply rooted in the cultural heritage of the islands, reflecting centuries-old traditions, techniques, and artistic expressions passed down through generations. From weaving and pottery to woodcarving and basketry, Cape Verdean artisans showcase their creativity, craftsmanship, and ingenuity in producing a wide range of handmade goods that serve both practical and decorative purposes.

One of the most iconic traditional crafts in Cape Verde is weaving, particularly of colorful textiles known as "panos" or "panuelos." Made from locally sourced cotton, wool, or silk, these intricately woven fabrics feature vibrant patterns and designs inspired by Cape Verdean culture, nature, and folklore. Women artisans, known as "tecelãs," skillfully weave panos on handlooms, creating textiles that are used for clothing, home décor, and ceremonial purposes.

Pottery is another traditional craft practiced in Cape Verde, with artisans shaping clay into functional and decorative objects such as pots, bowls, and figurines. The pottery tradition in Cape Verde dates back centuries, with techniques and styles influenced by African, European, and indigenous cultures. Artisans often use natural materials such as clay, sand, and ash to create pottery, firing the pieces in traditional kilns or open-air pits to achieve unique colors and textures.

Woodcarving is also a prominent traditional craft in Cape Verde, with artisans carving intricate designs and motifs into locally sourced woods such as mahogany, cedar, and olive. Common woodcarving techniques include relief carving, sculptural carving, and decorative carving, with artisans creating a variety of objects such as masks, sculptures, furniture, and musical instruments. Woodcarving in Cape Verde often incorporates symbolic imagery and cultural themes, reflecting the rich history and heritage of the islands.

Basketry is another traditional craft practiced by Cape Verdean artisans, with women weaving baskets, mats, and other woven goods from natural fibers such as palm leaves, sisal, and straw. Basketry techniques vary across the islands, with artisans using different weaving patterns, shapes, and materials to create functional and decorative items for everyday use and special occasions. Basketry products in Cape Verde range from simple household items to intricately designed works of art that showcase the skill and creativity of the artisans.

Overall, traditional crafts and artisanal skills play a vital role in preserving Cape Verdean culture, heritage, and identity, providing a connection to the past while also serving as a source of income, pride, and community cohesion for artisans and their families. Through their craftsmanship and creativity, Cape Verdean artisans continue to contribute to the rich tapestry of cultural diversity and artistic expression in the islands, ensuring that traditional crafts remain an integral part of Cape Verdean life for generations to come.

Women in Cape Verdean Society

Women play a vital role in Cape Verdean society, contributing to every aspect of life on the islands, from family and community to politics and the economy. Throughout Cape Verde's history, women have faced unique challenges and opportunities shaped by cultural traditions, socioeconomic factors, and historical events.

In Cape Verdean culture, women are often regarded as the backbone of the family, assuming multiple roles as caregivers, homemakers, and nurturers. They are responsible for managing household affairs, raising children, and maintaining social ties within the community. Despite these domestic responsibilities, many Cape Verdean women also participate in the workforce, balancing family obligations with employment outside the home.

Education has played a crucial role in empowering Cape Verdean women and expanding their opportunities for personal and professional growth. Over the years, efforts to improve access to education for girls and women have led to significant gains in female literacy rates and educational attainment levels. Today, Cape Verdean women are active participants in

101

all levels of education, from primary schools to universities, pursuing careers in diverse fields such as education, healthcare, business, and government.

In recent decades, Cape Verdean women have made significant strides in the political arena, with increased representation in government and leadership positions. The adoption of gender quotas and affirmative action policies has helped to promote women's participation in politics and decision-making processes, leading to the election of female lawmakers, cabinet ministers, and even a female president. These advances reflect a growing recognition of the importance of gender equality and women's empowerment in Cape Verdean society.

Despite these achievements, challenges remain for women in Cape Verde, including gender-based violence, economic inequality, and limited access to healthcare and reproductive services. Cultural norms and societal expectations regarding gender roles and responsibilities continue to shape women's lives, influencing their choices, opportunities, and experiences.

Efforts to address these challenges and promote gender equality in Cape Verde are ongoing, with initiatives focused on legal reforms, social programs, and awareness-raising campaigns.

Organizations and advocacy groups dedicated to women's rights and empowerment work tirelessly to address issues such as domestic violence, gender discrimination, and women's health, advocating for policy changes and providing support services for those in need.

Overall, women in Cape Verdean society play diverse and multifaceted roles, contributing to the country's social, economic, and political development in myriad ways. Through their resilience, determination, and solidarity, Cape Verdean women continue to shape the future of their families, communities, and nation, embodying the spirit of strength, courage, and perseverance that defines the essence of Cape Verdean womanhood.

Sports and Recreation: Cape Verdean Athletic Achievements

Sports and recreation hold a special place in Cape Verdean culture, serving as a source of pride, unity, and national identity for its people. While the islands may be small in size, their athletic achievements have garnered attention on both regional and international stages, showcasing the talent, dedication, and passion of Cape Verdean athletes.

One of the most popular sports in Cape Verde is football (soccer), which enjoys widespread participation and support across the islands. Football matches are a common sight in villages, towns, and cities, with local clubs competing in leagues and tournaments organized by the Cape Verdean Football Federation. Cape Verdean footballers have gained recognition for their skill and prowess, with some players going on to compete professionally in Europe and other parts of the world.

Basketball is also a beloved sport in Cape Verde, with a growing number of enthusiasts and amateur leagues popping up across the islands. Cape Verdean basketball players have made their mark in international competitions, representing the country with pride and distinction on the global stage. The sport has become a symbol of unity and camaraderie, bringing together players and fans from diverse backgrounds to celebrate their shared love of the game.

In addition to football and basketball, Cape Verdeans also excel in athletics, boxing, and martial arts, with athletes competing in regional and international events with notable success. Cape Verdean athletes have won medals and accolades in disciplines such as track and field, boxing, judo, and karate, earning recognition for their talent, determination, and sportsmanship.

The natural beauty and geography of Cape Verde provide ample opportunities for outdoor recreation and adventure sports. With its rugged landscapes, pristine beaches, and crystal-clear waters, the islands offer ideal conditions for activities such as surfing, windsurfing, kiteboarding, and snorkeling. Adventure seekers flock to Cape Verde to explore its diverse ecosystems, hike its volcanic peaks, and embark on eco-tours to discover its unique flora and fauna.

In recent years, Cape Verde has also emerged as a destination for sports tourism, attracting visitors from around the world to participate in events such as marathons, triathlons, and sailing regattas. The islands' warm climate, stunning scenery, and welcoming hospitality make them an ideal setting for sports enthusiasts seeking new challenges and unforgettable experiences.

Overall, sports and recreation play a central role in Cape Verdean society, fostering a sense of community, pride, and belonging among its people. Whether competing on the field, exploring the great outdoors, or cheering from the sidelines, Cape Verdeans embrace sports as a way to celebrate their culture, showcase their talents, and inspire future generations to pursue their dreams.

Education System: Nurturing Future Generations

The education system in Cape Verde is a cornerstone of the nation's development, playing a vital role in nurturing future generations and empowering individuals to reach their full potential. From early childhood education to tertiary institutions, Cape Verde's educational landscape is diverse, dynamic, and continually evolving to meet the needs of its population.

Primary education in Cape Verde is compulsory and free for children aged 6 to 12 years, providing a foundational education in core subjects such as mathematics, language arts, science, and social studies. Primary schools are distributed across the islands, with efforts made to ensure access to education for all children, regardless of geographical location or socioeconomic status. The curriculum is standardized nationwide, with emphasis placed on literacy, numeracy, and critical thinking skills.

Secondary education in Cape Verde encompasses both lower secondary (ages 12 to 15) and upper secondary (ages 15 to 18) levels, offering students the opportunity to pursue further studies and specialize in academic or technical fields. Lower secondary education builds upon the foundation laid in primary school, while upper secondary education provides students with the option to choose from academic or vocational tracks based on their interests and career aspirations.

Vocational education and training (VET) programs are an integral part of Cape Verde's education system, offering students practical skills and hands-on training in various trades and professions. VET programs are designed to prepare students for entry into the workforce or further education, providing pathways to careers in fields such as agriculture, construction, tourism, healthcare, and information technology. Cape Verdean youth have the opportunity to enroll in VET programs at specialized technical schools or vocational training centers located throughout the islands.

Higher education in Cape Verde is provided by universities, colleges, and institutes offering undergraduate and graduate degree programs in a wide range of disciplines. The University of Cape Verde (UNICV) is the largest and most prestigious institution of higher learning in the country, offering degree programs in fields such as education, engineering, business, law, and social sciences. In addition to UNICV, several private universities and colleges operate in Cape Verde, providing diverse educational opportunities for students seeking higher education.

The government of Cape Verde has made significant investments in education in recent years, with a focus on expanding access to quality education, improving teacher training, and enhancing the overall quality of learning outcomes. Efforts to modernize the education system include the integration of technology in classrooms, the development of e-learning platforms, and the implementation of educational reforms aimed at promoting innovation, creativity, and lifelong learning.

Despite progress made in recent decades, challenges remain in Cape Verde's education system, including issues related to access, equity, and quality. Rural and underserved communities often face barriers to accessing education due to factors such as geographic isolation, limited infrastructure, and socioeconomic disparities. Additionally, the quality of education varies across regions, with urban areas generally having better-equipped schools and more qualified teachers than rural areas.

Overall, the education system in Cape Verde is a dynamic and evolving sector that plays a critical role in shaping the future of the nation. By investing in the education and development of its youth, Cape Verde seeks to build a skilled workforce, promote social mobility, and foster sustainable economic growth and development for generations to come.

Healthcare System: Ensuring Well-being for All

The healthcare system in Cape Verde is a fundamental component of the country's social infrastructure, aimed at ensuring the well-being and health of its population. While the islands face unique challenges in delivering healthcare services due to their geographic isolation and limited resources, efforts have been made to provide accessible and quality healthcare to all residents.

The Ministry of Health oversees the healthcare system in Cape Verde, responsible for setting policies, regulations, and standards for healthcare delivery across the islands. The government allocates a significant portion of its budget to healthcare, investing in infrastructure, medical equipment, and human resources to support the delivery of essential health services.

Primary healthcare serves as the foundation of Cape Verde's healthcare system, with a network of health centers and clinics located throughout the islands, providing preventive, promotive, and curative care to individuals and families. Primary healthcare services include routine check-ups, vaccinations, prenatal care, family planning, and treatment for common illnesses and injuries.

Hospitals in Cape Verde provide secondary and tertiary healthcare services, offering specialized medical care, diagnostic procedures, and emergency treatment to patients with complex health needs. The largest hospital in Cape Verde is Agostinho Neto Hospital in Praia, equipped with modern facilities and medical professionals trained in various specialties.

Despite progress made in expanding healthcare access, challenges remain in Cape Verde's healthcare system, including issues related to healthcare infrastructure, medical equipment, and human resources. Rural and remote areas often lack access to adequate healthcare facilities and services, leading to disparities in health outcomes between urban and rural populations.

In recent years, efforts have been made to address these challenges through initiatives focused on strengthening healthcare infrastructure, improving medical equipment and supplies, and enhancing the training and recruitment of healthcare professionals. Partnerships with international organizations and foreign governments have also played a role in supporting healthcare development in Cape Verde.

One of the key priorities of Cape Verde's healthcare system is the promotion of public health and disease prevention. The Ministry of Health implements public health programs aimed at addressing prevalent health issues such as communicable diseases, non-communicable diseases, maternal and child health, and environmental health hazards. These programs focus on health education, awareness-raising, and community engagement to empower individuals and communities to adopt healthy behaviors and lifestyles.

In conclusion, the healthcare system in Cape Verde is a vital component of the country's social fabric, striving to ensure the well-being and health of its population. Despite challenges, efforts to strengthen healthcare infrastructure, expand access to services, and promote public health continue to improve health outcomes and contribute to the overall development of the nation.

Future Prospects: Cape Verde's Role on the Global Stage

As Cape Verde looks to the future, its role on the global stage is poised for growth and significance in various sectors. With its strategic location in the Atlantic Ocean, stable political environment, and commitment to development, Cape Verde has the potential to become a key player in regional and international affairs.

One area where Cape Verde is expected to make strides is in sustainable development and renewable energy. The country has abundant renewable energy resources, including wind, solar, and ocean energy, which can be harnessed to reduce reliance on fossil fuels and promote environmental sustainability. Cape Verde has already made significant investments in renewable energy projects, such as wind farms and solar power plants, and aims to further expand its renewable energy capacity in the coming years.

In addition to renewable energy, Cape Verde's strategic location makes it a natural hub for maritime trade and transportation. The country's ports and harbors serve as important transit points for shipping routes between Europe, Africa, and the Americas, offering opportunities for trade, commerce, and economic growth.

With proper infrastructure development and investment, Cape Verde can enhance its position as a maritime gateway and logistics hub in the Atlantic region.

Tourism is another area with immense potential for growth in Cape Verde. The country's pristine beaches, diverse landscapes, and rich cultural heritage attract visitors from around the world seeking sun, sand, and adventure. With increasing interest in sustainable and eco-friendly tourism, Cape Verde has the opportunity to develop its tourism industry in a responsible and environmentally conscious manner, preserving its natural beauty and cultural authenticity while generating revenue and employment opportunities for local communities.

Cape Verde's diaspora community also plays a significant role in the country's future prospects. Cape Verdeans living abroad contribute remittances, investment, and expertise to their homeland, supporting economic development and social progress. The government of Cape Verde has implemented policies to engage with the diaspora and leverage their resources and networks for the benefit of the country, fostering partnerships and collaborations in various fields.

On the international stage, Cape Verde actively participates in regional and global forums, advocating for issues such as climate change, sustainable development, and ocean conservation. As a small island developing state, Cape Verde faces unique challenges related to climate change and environmental sustainability, and seeks to work with other countries and organizations to address these challenges and build resilience.

Overall, Cape Verde's future prospects are bright, with opportunities for growth and development in various sectors. By leveraging its natural resources, strategic location, and human capital, Cape Verde can position itself as a dynamic and thriving nation on the global stage, contributing to regional stability, economic prosperity, and sustainable development for years to come.

Epilogue

In this journey through the vibrant tapestry of Cape Verde, we've explored the islands' rich history, diverse cultures, stunning landscapes, and promising future prospects. From the colonial roots that shaped its identity to the modern developments paving the way forward, Cape Verde stands as a testament to resilience, innovation, and the human spirit.

As we conclude our exploration, it's evident that Cape Verde is more than just a collection of islands; it's a dynamic nation with a unique blend of influences, traditions, and aspirations. From the bustling streets of Praia to the tranquil shores of Maio, each island offers its own distinct charm and allure, beckoning travelers to discover its hidden treasures.

Cape Verde's cultural heritage is a testament to the resilience and creativity of its people, who have preserved and celebrated their traditions through music, dance, cuisine, and storytelling. From the haunting melodies of morna to the energetic rhythms of funaná, Cape Verdean music embodies the soul of the islands, weaving together influences from Africa, Europe, and the Americas.

The islands' natural beauty is equally captivating, with pristine beaches, rugged mountains, and lush valleys waiting to be explored. Whether hiking through Santo Antão's verdant landscapes, diving in the crystal-clear waters of Sal, or stargazing atop Fogo's volcanic peaks, Cape Verde offers endless opportunities for adventure and discovery.

Looking ahead, Cape Verde's future is filled with promise and potential. With investments in renewable energy, tourism, education, and healthcare, the country is poised to build a brighter and more sustainable future for its people. As it continues to engage with the global community, Cape Verde will play an increasingly important role in regional and international affairs, contributing its unique perspective and expertise to address global challenges.

But perhaps the true essence of Cape Verde lies in its people – resilient, resourceful, and deeply connected to their land and culture. Despite facing challenges, Cape Verdeans possess an unwavering spirit of optimism and determination, forging ahead with hope and determination to create a better tomorrow for themselves and future generations.

As we bid farewell to Cape Verde, let us carry with us the memories of its beauty, the warmth of its people, and the lessons learned from its journey. May we be inspired to embrace diversity, cherish our heritage, and work together to build a more inclusive and sustainable world for all. Until we meet again, saudade, Cape Verde.

Printed in Great Britain
by Amazon

56411486R10066